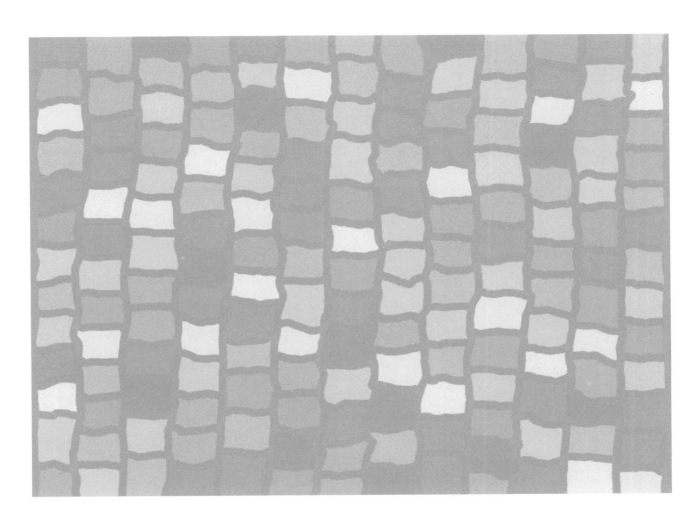

an era of abc rhymes

isbn: 9781088070901

to all the dreamers and all the lovers...

A is for the afterglow and all too well you say

all the girls you loved before said all you had to do was stay

if august was your anti-hero, 10 minutes will unfurl

a perfectly good heart can misplace a place in this world

B is breathless and bejeweled, it's better than revenge,
bad blood with some beautiful ghosts can spark begin again
if betty went back to december say bye bye baby, bye
she'd breathe into the blank space that's bigger than the whole sky
a better man can come along, she'll let him call her babe
and james would never do her wrong, her heart would never break

C is for change, that's crazier than a christmas tree farm

but call it what you want to with that carolina charm

i'll clean my champagne problems, to not be as cold as you

that coney island closure, you're a cowboy like me too

left your old cardigan somewhere, that is the biggest bummer

i'd say come back, be here, but that would be a real cruel summer

you'd come in with the rain like we were on cornelia street

but castles crumbling shut that door and we will not repeat

D is death by a thousand cuts when dear john left me in that dress

that daylight came so delicate, sore debut i must confess,

dorothea, don't you, don't blame me, dear reader knows who lied

that grip he had, like we were stuck, dancing with our hands tied

E is the great epiphany, now everything has changed

our eyes open for evermore and lead to this end game

the exile ended slowly, now enchanted just as much

as the first time that we met and i felt your electric touch

E is a little foolish one, like when you are fifteen
a false god brings forever winter if we stay naive
but we can be the fearless ones and always stand our ground
we'll forever & always sing our folklore all around

G is for the gorgeous glitch,

a fate getaway car,

a girl at home with a gold rush,

transcribed in every star

7

H is this haunted place, that lost its happiness

hey steven, say this ain't a hoax, it hits different, i stress

and this is how you get the girl to transform what you found

turning high infidelity into a holy ground

8

I is for innocent things i heart? at least, i almost do,

i think he knows that i know places, where i can see you

it feels like i did something bad, not like illicit affairs,

but i knew you were trouble, is it over now? ivy cares

invisible, it's time to go, i bet you think about me,

i wish you would be tied to me with an invisible string

i'm only me when i'm with you, if this was a movie, the end

i forgot that you existed but it's nice to have a friend

is jealous, burning red
but joyous when you call
you're in over your head again
you always jump then fall

K is for karma, but of course

it come right back around

one day you're the king of my heart

the next i take the crown

L is for the love story, that last kiss that we shared

long story short, that london boy went running away, scared

this lover labyrinth won't long live, stuck in this purple maze

look what you made me do, i axed it to lavender haze

M is the mad woman you left driving my mastermind

you dream of marjorie, like in mary's song, oh my my my

i stare at your mean maroon eyes, mr. perfectly fine

and realize that the midnight rain hasn't stopped since you've been mine

your hate is like a mirrorball, push any faults away

but i don't let that inside me! all my tears ricochet

we were miss americana & the heartbreak prince, you see

but we're a message in a bottle sinking in memory

N is nothing new, you never grow up quite in time
on new year's day you killed me but there's no body, no crime
now that we don't talk, a memory, just like nineteen eighty-nine
it's time that new romantics take care of this heart of mine

is ours, and only the young

can lead us out of the woods

we sing our song with words

that no one else has understood

P is the peace we found in paris

crafting paper rings

don't need one more picture to burn

with you my heart just sings

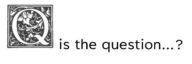is the question...?

or it was...or is it? will it be...?

you'll never know unless you ask,

i guess we'll wait and see

17

is the setting sun's red glow, there someone by the sea

i run to ronan on the beach but it's just a memory

i always think i'm ready for it? how can i ever be

the reputation of this grief is no stranger to me

a smile, a tear, they come to me i welcome what i see

you'll be forever in my heart, i'm right where you left me

S is sweeter than fiction, like superman in flight

to catch you so you're safe and sound and shake it off by night

when some called you "slut!" at seven, you should've said no

return that cruel unwanted gift, soon you'll get better though

you say don't go but sagittarius smiles in the night sky

suburban legends tell us that it's time to say goodbye

like seeing some snow on the beach, wishing it stay stay stay

the sad beautiful tragic sun melts the beauty away

that sweet nothing in september, that state of grace that you speak now

but nothing will stay beautiful forever, can it, how?

if starlight becomes out of style that's something no one knows

superstar bursts and sparks fly down, well then... so it goes...

T is for the timeless songs we sang out by the lakes

the last time you said i'm the 1, that was your first mistake

i think that i was 22, that's when, the very first night

this love was tied together with a smile, the best day in my sight

i thought today was a fairytale and the way i loved you was strong

i was the lucky one living in a tim mcgraw love song

you were the man, the archer, tell me why you shot my heart

and left teardrops on my guitar, the great war broke apart

and that was the moment i knew the outside is where i would stay

in the story of us, this is me trying to say

this is why we can't have nice things, tolerate it no more

cuz 'tis the damn season for slamming the other side of the door

the last great american dynasty is how we felt then, but now dead

this treacherous love memory is all that's left within my head

20

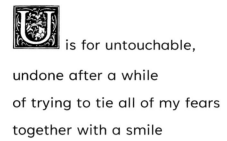is for untouchable,

undone after a while

of trying to tie all of my fears

together with a smile

V is for the voice memos
i heard and caught your lies
i'm on my vigilante shit
and you're on coward cries

W is wonderland from all my wildest dreams

when we were happy, like a willow dancing in the breeze

but then you welcome to new york all of those girls somehow

so we are never ever getting back together now

we would've, could've, should've but no white horse is enough

to make me feel what emma feels when emma falls in love

X will always mark the spot
that was the place we split
no getaway cars ever saved
our chances to fix it

24

is all about you, and you belong with me

but you're not sorry and i'm stuck, with you all over me

you need to calm down, you don't care, you're losing me today

you're on your own, kid, even though you are in love, you say

Z is for your buddy zayn, who sings with you to say
that i don't want to live forever, but enjoy here, today
but don't catch zzz's and don't you dare sleep on my homegirl tay
cuz her name and rep will bring on some more era rhymes one day

...for now

Printed in the USA
CPSIA information can be obtained
at www.ICGtesting.com
LVHW060221251123

764788LV00020B/1408